Advance Praise
When There Were No Borders

Sánchez writes borderless in borderless times. He breaks through the ancient Mexica figure of death and transformation, Coatlicue, to poems as pyramids, to the Sea of the Salish in the Pacific Northwest and on to cool-rebel Pachuco dialect of the US-Mexico borderlands. He cooks on a rotating rainbow-colored pan, he spices, he refuses to present his "papers" at the border stop. There are nectars, harvests, the always-farmworker fields, a detention center to tend to with resources and a poet. Open this collection — hold on, there is a "pirinola," an ever spinning umbrella-shaped candy with a pointed tip burning colors, lights and stories that will take you to Latinx multi-dimensional magic. A precise, moving mural, this text of visitations of "life, precious life!" Sanchez's delights as he writes, as he tears across those borderlines, dancing. Magnificent poetics to take home and to take you out.

— Juan Felipe Herrera
Poet Laureate of the United States Emeritus

Raúl Sánchez's long-awaited 2nd book is a gift, a gateway, a harvest. These poems present and re-present our "tongue," our "language," our "culture and pride." Steeped in history and "blood blood blood" unforgotten and dignified, these poems are never what you expect yet are as familiar as an ancestral landscape. Deeply layered like culture itself, this book es una flor, multi-petalled, many-voiced — sin frontera and utterly unique. From rich love poems to Nerudaesque declamaciónes to canciones and cantos, this book represents as we were, and are, *When There Were No Borders*, by presenting the multiverse that is US of America through the voice of one, Raúl Sánchez, crossing borders.

— Lorna Dee Cervantes
Chicana poet and activist
Author of *EMPLUMADA, DRIVE, CIENTO...*

These versos harken back to the original masters of the movimiento. Raúl Sánchez reminds me why I started writing poems so long ago. They burn with witness and life.

– Luis Alberto Urrea
author of *The House of Broken Angels*

In "Before There Were Borders" poet Raúl Sánchez carves for us an especially didactic milagro with gleaming Mexican cultural lessons in verse. Since the 1960's Chicanx poets have hailed the Pre-Columbian Gods and Goddesses. He enters this arena expanding the traditional pantheon of deities, stimulating the young and the old, the Chicano youth and Northwest populations alike, (Latinx almost 12 per cent of Washington state population). His poetry is for the woke and those who want to wake up. It is current and inscribes us in the historical border and its porosity, for a man who learned English as a child and reflects for us through his magical words, the richness of interstitial territories of mind and land, for the last fifty years.

– Gabriella Gutiérrez y Muhs
Poet and Professor, Departments of Modern Languages
and Women Gender & Sexuality Studies, Seattle University

Light, sound, and language create paths of profound depth and compassion in this collection of poetry. As symbols and languages intertwine, a dancing spectrum of experiences shines from the many stories and images of these poems like light through a prism. "Tonight, I find myself sewing memories," writes the poet, and each poem in this collection is stitched with care and suffused with vitality, urgency, and beauty.

– Laura Da'
Author of *Tributaries*, winner of the American Book Award

I know Raúl Sánchez best as a poet colleague working in juvenile detention, an experience that Sánchez conveys in several poems. In one he describes these youth poems as "gems, strung together like diamonds, after the rain." I apply that image to the poems in this book, too. Sánchez begins with poems about his Mexican childhood – his mother making tortillas, and the clap of her hands. He moves on to poems about his family's relationship to America, such as his father's work as a bracero during World War II. Then there are poems about Sánchez's Mexican-American experience, including being subjected to bigotry; and finally there are poems about Sánchez's Pacific Northwest home. In all, these poems are gems that are beautiful as a strand because they originate in Sánchez's open heart, and they glitter with his honesty, clarity, and sense of discovery.

– Richard Gold
Founder of the Pongo Poetry Project

WHEN THERE WERE NO BORDERS

FLOWERSONG
PRESS

POEMS BY
Raúl Sánchez / Tlaltecatl

FLOWERSONG
PRESS

FlowerSong Press
Copyright © 2021 by Raúl Sánchez
ISBN: 978-1-953447-65-4
Library of Congress Control Number: 2021940939

Published by FlowerSong Press
in the United States of America.
www.flowersongpress.com

"Espíritus caminando en el río" by Fulgencio Lazo
Graphic Art by René Julio
Cover Design by Priscilla Celina Suarez
Set in Adobe Garamond Pro

Thank you to the City of Redmond.

WHEN THERE WERE NO BORDERS

POEMS BY

Raúl Sánchez / Tlaltecatl

PRAYER OF THANKS
By Chief Sealth

Every part of this Earth is sacred,
every shining pine needle,
every sandy shore,
every thing in the dark woods;

teach your children that the Earth is our Mother
as, whatever befalls the Earth, befalls the children of the Earth.
We are part of the Earth, and the Earth is part of us and,
we belong to the Earth.

This we know, "All things are connected".
Like the blood which unites one family, all things are connected,
for we did not weave the web of life.
We are merely a strand in it.

Whatever we do to the web, we do to ourselves and to our children.
Let us give thanks for the web and the Circle that connects us all.

Muchísimas gracias!

Above all, I want to thank Edward Vidaurre for asking me to submit my manuscript, and for all his calls for submissions through Facebook as well as other media. I'd like to thank Jo Reyes-Boitel for her suggestions and insight editing my manuscript. Thank you to my wife Heather who is always my first reader. I'd like to express my deep appreciation to Laura LeHew Poet/Editor for catching my punctuation errors and oversights.

Thank you to Richard Gold from PONGO Teen Writing for including me as one of the writing volunteers mentoring youth in detention. I'm very grateful to the Seattle Arts and Lectures Writers In The Schools (WITS) program, and the Jack Straw Cultural Center for including me as a dual language poetry mentor.

To the City of Redmond and the Arts and Culture Commission for giving me the opportunity to represent the city as their 2019-2021 Poet Laureate. To the City of Shoreline Cultural and Community Services as well as the City of Burien Arts Commission To Tieton Arts and Humanities.

To Luis Samuel Santiago Melchor, (Yolkapoli Tlajkuiloani), for helping me with the Nahuatl translations. To Fulgencio Lazo, whose art speaks poetry in color and movement. To Dra. Gabriella Gutiérrez y Muhs for including me in her projects. To artist Rene Julio for his skillful work. To all poets and friends who have inspired and encouraged me to continue planting poetic seeds in the minds of the youth.

This book was made possible by the City of Redmond Arts and Culture Commission.

ACKNOWLEDGEMENTS

I thank the editors of the journals and on-line publications in which some of these poems at times in slightly different form have appeared.

Viva la Word Anthology "Colors of Life" (English version only)

Subprimal Poetry Art/Music Issue 1 on-line 2013 "Mexica Tiahui"

Pirene's Fountain 2013 "Smoke" "Kumbh Mela for the Crows"

Redmond Association of Spokenword Poetry Anthology Here, There, and Everywhere "Smoke"

The Raven Chronicles "Salsa Verde"

Clover "Maguey Spines", "Land of Dreams"

Texas Poetry Calendar 2016 and *2018* "Incarnated / Encarnada"

Pirene's Fountain, Vol 4, Issue 9, April 2011 Translation of "El correr de los años" - "The Passing of the Years" by Renato Leduc in Obra Literaria, 2000 Fondo de Cultura Económica.

La Bloga "Behind the Barbed Wire", "Wind"

Anacua Literary Arts Journal "Border Crossing"

Cutthroat, Puro Chicanix Writers of the 21st Century "Show me Your Papers"

Poets Unite! Litfuse @10 Anthology "Vines and Wind"

The Smoking Poet "The Shelter of your Chest"

Between The Lines, Edmonds Community College Art and Literary Magazine "Two Boats"

Lowriting, shots, rides and stories from the Chicano Soul, Broken Sword Publications "Quemando llanta", "Reminiscing", "Chevy Impala"

Footbridge Above the Falls, Rose Alley Press "Found Sonnets"

wa.poeticroutes.com "Tieton's Bounty"

Burien Magazine "Bountiful Burien"

Lake City Memorial Public Art "Life Precious Life!"

City of Shoreline Cultural and Community Services Public Art and on-line project "Vertebrae" - "Vertebras" Play Ball (COVID-19), "Play Ball!" - "¡Pleibol!", "Smothered by Nature" – "Sofocado por la naturaleza", "Ode to and Oak Tree" – "Oda a un roble viejo", "Greensward" – "Césped"

Boundless, Fall Special Anthology "Ode to an Avocado","This Poem Doesn't Exist"

FOR HEATHER AND MARINA, EL CORAZÓN Y EL ALMA DE MI VIDA.

Contents

IV •••• THE PACIFIC NORTHWEST

Let there be everywhere our voices, our eyes, our thoughts, our love, our actions, breathing hope and victory.

-- Sonia Sánchez, African American Poet

Part I • ce

Achto' pa / antes / before

ORIGINS

Itlapaltin nemiliztli

xiknechmachati, nemiliztli!
chichiltik uikpa tlakatilistli iuan estli
in texotli – xoxoktiiuik iluikatlampa
iuan in ueyameh
kostik tlasohtla in tonatiu iuan ikoxisentli
kamiltitlalli, atoctli
lalaxtletl, tlaixpoloani, maciticayotl
teixtlaltemiani, poktli mochiua
in youalli iuan in mictlan
santepan,
istaiuiomimeh iuan tlakuepalistli

5

Colores de la vida
(Inspirado por el significado Maya de los colores)

Muéstrame la vida!
Rojo de sangre y nacimiento
Azul-verde de los cielos
Y los océanos
Amarillo como el sol y el maíz tierno
Café de la tierra y los campos fértiles
Anaranjado como el fuego destructor
Purificante
El cegador humo gris
Se convierte
En la obscuridad de la noche
Y el inframundo
Finalmente,
El blanco de los huesos y el cambio.

Colors of Life
(Inspired by the Mayan significance of color)

Show me, life!
Red for birth and blood
Blue–green of the heavens
And the oceans
Yellow like the sun and ripe corn
Brown earth, fertile pastures
Orange fire, destroyer, purifier
Blinding gray smoke becomes
The blackness of the night and the underworld
Finally,
White of bones and change.

Mexica Tiahui

I
walked
the steps where
priests, Zapotec kings, left
footprints rituals performed
to invisible gods. Mictlantecuhtli,
Mictlantecihuatl, rulers of the underworld
and all living things. Their energy emanating
through temple stones carved, shaped vestiges of
reverence to nature, culture found two centuries before
the Spanish arrived these standing monuments proof of our
undefeated spirit and struggle: Zapotec, Toltec, Olmec, Mayan,
Aztec cultures proof to the world that our ancestors were intelligent
people, knowledgeable, cultured, devout beings in harmony with the
universe, life and death. The sun shines its light upon us as we
follow the moon path to rivers where we will survive, we will never perish.

Cintéotl

Goddess of corn grown
from earth, rain and sun
kernels boiled nixtamal
grinding corn into dough
amasando
smoothing the dough

her soft hands soften the masa
grabbing a handful
left hand to right hand
begin to clap, clap, clap
from one damp hand to the other
her fingers stiff

with the slightest cup
and spring to the palm
clap and turn, clap and turn
lay it on the comal
flipped over
to cook the other side—

my mother's hands,
her spirit evoked
when I cook
aroma of fresh tortillas
fragrant and moist
remembering the sound

of her hands,
clap and turn,
clap and turn.

Mexicayotl / Mexicanity

Nahuatl, Maya, Zapoteco, Mixteco
Otomí, Tzeltal, Tzotzil, Totonaca
Mazateco, Chol, Mazahua, Huasteco
Chinanteco, Purépecha, Mixe, Mayo

Tlapaneco, Tarahumara, Zoque, Tojolabal
Chontal, Popoluca, Chatino, Amuzgo
Huichol, Tepehuán, Triqui, Popoloca
Cora, Canjobal, Yaqui, Cuicateco

Mame, Huave, Tepehua, Pame
Chontal, Choj, Chichimeca, Guarijío
Matlatzinca, Kekchí, Chocholteca
Pima, Jalalteco, Ocuilteco, Seri, Quiché

Ixcateco, Cakchiquel, Kikapú,
Motozintleco, Paipai, Kumiai, Ixil
Pápago, Cucapá, Cochimí, Lacandón
Kiliwa, Teco, Aguacateco.

Flanked by an ocean and a gulf called México
entre un océano y un golfo llamado México
jungle to the south
la selva en el sur

and the ever-growing wall
y el muro que sigue creciendo
to the north – protected,
en el norte – protegido.

Tepeilhuitl

Harvest time when the souls come in.
Thirteenth month of the Aztec calendar.

Festival of the Mountains and Tlaloc,
god of rain and thunder.

Pathway for the souls to follow on their return.
Miquiztli, death; facing north, Mictlampa.

The souls are coming — along with Ehécatl, wind.
We sweep the graves, the front porch.

We spread marigold petals out the door.
Técpatli, flintstone, Océlotl, jaguar also facing north.

Manifest to remind us life is a cycle and every year
The dormant souls travel to the Calli, home,

where they lived before.
From the Mictlān they arrive, hungry and thirsty.

Our offering, humble or sumptuous,
will help them settle in, to enjoy all we have to give.

When we call their names to remember them,
and feel their presence once again.

My Tongue / Mi lengua

My tongue retains the roaring sound of rivers, of the earth after the rain falling over leaves, branches and flowers.

My tongue is stained with the juice of sweet pitayas, red, delicious, grown under Tonatiuh's rays, our father sun.

My tongue reveres nature and all living beings, mountains, rivers, oceans, night and day.
My tongue wears Quetzal feathers mystical birds from the Mayan paradise.

My tongue is impregnated with Calpulli, Tonalli, Xochitl, Xochipilli, Mictlantecuhtli, Cuauthemoc, Moctezuma, Quetzalcoatl, Tomatl, Centeotl.

My tongue speaks of temples, demigods, copal, flowers, medicinal plants, jade masks, golden pectorals, obsidian stones, volcanoes, and blood.

My ancient tongue speaks Zapotec, Nahuatl, Purépecha, Tzotzil, Otomi, Chamula, Mayan, Tarahumara.

My tongue is my identity—the connection to my people, my roots, my culture.
My language is from the earth, from the heavens, from my soul.

My tongue speaks, my soul feels the breath of the earth, the sound of the wind Ehecatl.

My tongue, my language,
My culture and pride.

Smoke
A tribute to Grandma Carmen

When I was a young child, my Grandmother cleansed my body,
with herbs and smoke.

She swiftly brushed my body with ramas de pirul and flowers
red ribbon held,

the willow branches she brushed, brushed,
brushed away.

my stretched limbs — bad energy away
from me.

Fragrant sap remained on fingers dark
from cutting,

herbs frankincense chunks
burning copal—

Top, down, left, right her eyes closed.
Cleansing smoke.

Branches swirled the smoke,
with every stroke—

shaking filtering negative energy
the room full of smoke—

cleansing smoke
chasing evil spells—

silent prayer whisper
echoed, through the smoke,

she opened her eyes
two moons behind the clouds.

She wrapped the loaded branches
told me to throw them, behind my back—

and walk away—
into the light.

Salsa Verde

Mother roasted
tomatillos whole
serranos, onion
on *comal* stove top
pungent air permeated
swells of flavor

tomatillos turned yellow
with dark burnt spots
time for her hands to grind
tomatillos, *chiles* with mortar
salt chunks, garlic, clove
fresh cilantro, crushing, crushing

blending, turning mortar churning
delicious salsa on *molcajete*
grinding stone
steamy spicy smell
tickled my nose
spicy pleasure

eaten on tortillas, tostadas
my tongue on fire
oh man!
give me more.
I'll wash it down with Tequila
gift from the gods

Mother's salsa
made on *molcajete*
grinding stone.

Mi libertad

Soy   un   marinero   de   medianoche
cuyos   sueños   crecen   en   la   niebla
y   se   d e s p l o m a n   en   la   alborada.

Mis   pensamientos cuelgan
como   c u e r d a s   anudadas
m i d i e n d o   su   apertura

por
debajo
de
las
sabanas.

El sentimiento familiar
me   m a n t i e n e   en   mi   lugar.

Su   propio   peso   los   mantendrá
tensos   y   desenredados.

Me   alegra   la   libertad
de   mi   propia   voluntad.

Tengo   un   buen   sentido
de   mis   prácticas   distorsionadas.

Algunas   p e r s o n a s   piensan

que   soy   un   l u n á t i c o,
pero   en   realidad

soy
un   marinero   de
medianoche.

Milagros

Have you ever pinned down
a *milagro* on the cloth

of your favorite saint?
Tiny silver and brass charms offered

to thank for blessings received.
A house for the broken home,

A split heart for lost love,
praying for the lover to come back.

A hand for the injured laborer,
or the writer that can't write.

A mouth for those who speak
ill words praying they'll heal.

A foot to complete the journey,
to be able to move around,

Un-confined un-assisted.
A body for the departed,

or for the living wishing
they'd come home safe,

after deployment
to wars on foreign lands.

And the migrants
crossing deserts,

to arrive safe
to the promised land.

Or their home
away from this world.

Milagros testimony of love
a promise of faith and hope.

Mole Poblano

Sixteenth Century, Puebla City
cultural crossroad
where the new and the old
world collided.

Legend says that a magical wind gust,
swept the precise proportion of spices
and condiments into *cazuelas de barro*
at the Santa Rosa convent.

Ancient *mexica* advice
using chocolate in splendorous ways
taken from the eldest Mayans
quintessential *mestizo* delicacy.

Roasting chiles *pasilla*, *mulato*
ancho, grinding cloves, cinnamon,
anise seeds, black pepper, garlic,
almonds, peanuts, raisins.

On *metate* grinding stone
gentle grind making the paste
with native Mayan chocolate
by gentle Mexican hands.

1960

Five years young or younger
I was standing, walking…
Black and white photos taken
now fading in the memory of my past—

Growing up at my Mom and Dad's
restaurant right next to the biggest—
bullfighting arena in the world,
Plaza México! where everything began.

Meanwhile, Jack Kerouac
getting high in my city.
Jazz poet, 242 Blues choruses written
in an afternoon jam session.

*"& I came back Spitting Pulque in Borracho Ork
Saloons of old Sour Aztec "Askin for more…"*

My father enrolled me in a private American School
Escuela Rikards from kindergarten to 5th grade.
My best friends then were Sally, Dick and Spot.
Scared of Santa Claus, learned about Halloween,

before I revered the Day of the Dead.
Once, I stole two hours from a day
I don't remember the week,
month or year, but I did it.

It was the day when I put the early bird songs
in my pocket after listening—
to the sound of young ladies,
clicking heels and castanets.

with amorous echoes nailed down—
to the soulless songs sung
by drunken patrons
at the restaurant my father owned—

where the jaguars don't stop
nor the wounded beggars
nor the condors descending
from the Andes higher peaks.

I stole two hours—
I filled them with roses, words,
feelings and metaphor
rhyme, and me—

above the subway
below the heavens
of this earth
where I stood still.

Television

Leading age baby-boomers like me witnessed
        history's perpetuity in black and white.
Television had everything I didn't know
        But I saw it, because it was there.

Merry Melodies and merry tunes
        Betty Boop and Felix the Cat
Bugs Bunny, Daffy Duck, Porky Pig, and Elmer Fudd.
        My young mind numbed with illusion.

I saw John F. Kennedy shot over and over,
        His head rocking back and forth.
I saw black athletes raise their black fists—
        to protest racism in America.

I saw Vietnam war soldiers spat on their face—
        Television had everything I didn't know.
I saw Neil Armstrong walk on the moon.
        MLK Jr. and John Lewis beaten across the bridge.

I saw anti-war protesters mistreated.
        Kent State students shot to death.
I saw Pelé win the World Cup.
        Bullfighters dead in the arena.

I saw the Saint Louis Cardinals win the World Series.
        Television had everything I needed to know.
I saw Salvador Allende killed by the CIA.
        Sandinistas fighting against Somoza.

I saw Fidel Castro tumble Fulgencio Batista.
        Mexican activists killed on the mountains of Guerrero.
I saw students massacred in Tlatelolco Square—
        Díaz Ordaz's dirty-war against el pueblo.

I saw everything I know, 65 years ago still latent, infantasized.
   Today I continue to raise my fist, I protest, I demand,
I proclaim, equality, respect for others, for the land,
   demanding respect for the working class.

I saw it all—

Maguey Spines
After Marty Matz (1934 – 2001)

Pot smoking poet immersed
in pipe dreams found on the outskirts
of dusty roads climbing hills dressed in
yellow leaves with rattle snake breath

and elephant dreams.
The green cocoons become butterflies
released by the seashore
where the shaman puts the jigsaw puzzle piece

back in the black hole we call sky
The monsoons, the monsoons, the monsoons
living water to dampen the quickest spirit
bring down the highest mind

thunderbird glyphs etched on bones.
Let those dreams swing wrapped in hammocks
gardenia fragrance too sweet for the tiger's claws
alchemy of love stitched on the butterfly jaws.

Hey lady, bring your ivory towers, plant your roots
next to the copulating earthworms by the temple doors
please unravel your cosmic eyes, let them cascade
down your shoulders to your lovely hips

my pendulum grows and glows from heart to ear
please ease my clocks inner frenzy
I'm hanging on the tips of maguey spines
where the skulls are pale

transfixed by the sunlight and the spinning mirrors
the rancid stench of putrid lives under the grey sky
Mexico's dirt and grime unexplored madness
only the stop light clowns know where to find.

Madness lurks and howls cloying thoughts
waiting for the green hummingbirds to break
the purple dawn and taste the sugar mountains
of the unknown along with the stones below.

*Marty traveled Mexico's empty roads moving backwards in time to find
Coca-Cola, Singer sewing machines and pool tables, he called them the
'unholy trinity' Marty dedicated poems to all he knew.*

Incarnated
After Frida Kahlo

Incarnated with rose petal lips
earth colored skin
eyes like midnight moons
flowers in her hair
like a star queen brilliant
shimmering
yellow aquamarine
emerging from earth
a fountain of hope
life, color, heat
art from eye to eye unbound
from eyebrow to eyebrow
born and created into the universe
among corn plants, husks
grown from the ground, our earth
brown as the color of her skin.

Encarnada
Para Frida Kahlo

Encarnada con labios
como pétalos de rosa
piel de la tierra
ojos de luna nocturna
flores en su cabello
como una reina estrella
deslumbrante
aguamarina amarilla
emergiendo de la tierra
como una fuente de aliento,
de vida, de calor, color
arte de ojo a ojo
de ceja a ceja y después
al universo nacida y creada
entre mazorcas y el maíz,
crecida de la tierra
morena como el color de su piel.

El correr de los años
- Renato Leduc 1897- 1986 México

No me alegro ni me asusto
por mi condición senil.
Vivo tranquilo y a gusto,
en diciembre y en abril…

Amiguitas y amigotes
me obsequian con su amistad.
Y aún no siento los brotes
de mortal enfermedad.

Con esfuerzo y con decoro,
oculto a ojos extraños,
el natural deterioro
que me han dejado los años.

El natural deterioro
de tantos y tantos años,
no se remedia con oro…
se aliviana con redaños.

Y es que se largan las cejas
mientras se pierde la vista.
Ya no te pelan las viejas
ni logras una conquista…

Mientras los huevos se alargan
mientras se acorta la pinga.
Esta largura te embarga,
y esa cortedad te chinga…

En las montañas del Norte
un labriego pontifica:
no se me achique ni acorte
ni se meta a la botica.

Y se te pican los dientes
y el cráneo luce pelón
"Ay, reata, no te revientes
que es el último jalón…"

Y se presenta la muerte,
un día tiene que llegar.
Y como ya no eres fuerte
al carajo; a descansar…

The Passing of the Years
by Renato Leduc translation by Raúl Sánchez

I'm not glad, nor scared
about my senile condition thing.
I live quiet and comfortable,
in winter and spring...

Lady friends and chums
give me the gift of their ease.
And yet I do not feel the outbreaks
of my deadly disease.

With effort and decorum,
from stranger eyes I keep
natural decay
passing years sneaked.

Natural decay I hold
of many, so many years,
can not be healed with gold...
it gets easier with guts not tears.

It all starts when the eyebrows elongate
while we loose our sight.
women don't give a damn
let alone a date ...

While your testicles lengthen
and your penis shortens.
The longing makes you sad,
and the shyness fucks you up...

In the northern mountains
a peasant pontificates:
"Do not belittle yourself or come up short
don't even think walking into a drug store."

And then your teeth rotten
and your skull looks bald
"Oh, I hope my rope won't snap
this is the last tug…"

Then death comes,
one day has to come.
And since you are no longer strong
to hell with it; sleep where you belong…

Ode to an Avocado

You!

Shaped like an ovum seed in the middle
of the branches hanging with all your brothers
and, perhaps your sisters.

Did you know that I've known you since I was five?
I really didn't   really   know   you   then
but I heard about you at that time.

You were presented, introduced in my mouth
as a mushy-soft, sometimes tangy-spicy-oniony-decadent
delicacy, served in small bowls and dipping dishes.

That soft green creamy buttery meat
sensation in my palate could not
identify the deliciousness under

the hard crusty skin that protects you.
Dark green as my midnight dreams, bumpy
as the cloudy days bereft of sun-light.

Where have you been? Oh, I see, hiding beneath
the bushel crates of transported, imported food
other immigrants harvested at the right time,

south of the equator where alpacas, mules, donkeys
and mountain goats go. Handled by those humble
brown skinned hands from faraway lands

where the sun shines brighter.
You are free! But trapped—
in a plastic mesh

with five other guys
your friends I presume, even though…
the sign says 4 in a pack.

Ahuacatl, is your name!
but nobody calls you that
I think I know why.

Behind the Barbed Wire

In the olden days
southwest folks lived free—
unbound along
dusty border towns

before
there was a fence
before
there was a wall—

now they live
fenced in
lined up
against the wall.

Land of Dreams

On the edge of my mind,
I have thoughts almost forgotten, questions—
I cannot ask to those who vanished, erased
from the landscape, from our presence.

That is why I am addressing you,
my friends, wherever you may be,
happy or sad.

I salute you from the green landscape,
flowery and rainy, where the twisted train tracks
intersect amidst the grown weeds and the morning mist.

I am approaching you, to ask you,
please tell me whether it is true or false
or at least —

whisper
as if it were midnight while listening to the sound
of the clock's ticking, or the distant train whistle,

if you think this is your world, your country,
your planet...

Turning around with the propulsion of your own blood.
Is this harmony that surrounds you?

Perhaps you have heard about the brutal protests
from those who like you, were treated like unwanted prisoners.

Shouted in desperation in the valleys, forests and fields
the birds, the sole witness that saw your small bodies

crossing the river, without drowning.
Your parents running into the vast terrain guided by spines

and bleached bones where the flagpole
is only a splintered stick—

Guided by the flight of birds and empty bottles
following traces of cattle and horses

they arrived—
an unknown region from where they never returned,

where they found—
the bridge to liberty.

Step-by-step over the bridge they found new doors
another language, another voice,

the light of union and progress
no longer dreaming but living the dream

unbound
under the star-spangled sky…
of freedom.
FREE!

Praise for the Walking Warriors

This   IS   for all the migrants!
The shoeless
The desperate
The risk takers
The caring fathers and mothers
The elders the young bloods
The babies
The laborers
The engineers
The aspiring writers!
The ones who want to get ahead
The humans with colored skins,
kissed by the sun
The ones who are no longer

dreaming—

The ones who know the land
The ones who harvest our fruits and vegetables
The ones who take care of our elders
The ones who cook our food
The ones who sing hymns and turn prayer wheels
The poor ones—
The unafraid
The women who were raped
The young women
who want their children
to have a better life
To all who desire
and strive
for Freedom!

Border Crossing

talking   twisted   tongue
    language   among   the   tundra
lichen   blackberry bushes   thorns

      holding   back   ripping   our   clothes
piercing   our   skin
        bleeding
     falling   off   the   leaves
      like   morning   dew
and   the   red   dawn—

    down   the   path

   the   fence   border   guards   dressed

     in   grey   grunt   **"stop"**
     don't   move!
  frozen   we   stayed   looking
bleeding   with
  the   birdsong   and   the sound
  of   dangling   keys
we   remained   anonymous—

no   papers   no   names   no   passports
  only   the   light   in   our   eyes
    to   cross   the   fence
cuffed   and   wet

behind   us   a   language   of   fear
  to   break   us   to   lay   us
    down
  under   the   darkened   sky

    the   distant   gunfire—
and   torture   screams
   we   stood   still
  by   the   fence   bleeding   in   fear

Show Me Your Papers

I will show you my papers.
Which ones first?
Old yellow papers dated 1944

My father's papers Atchinson Railway man
bracero hard work *con* pride
he worked here during the war

my *abuelo's* yellow pay stubs
from the Yuma farm scorching heat
Tío Manuel's pay stub too small

Imperial Valley lettuce land
what papers you want to see
first and last.

My ID driver license
legal document to move around?
My wedding certificate?

testimony to my wife—
and all my vows.
My kids birth certificates

born in this land.
Social Security card?
My paycheck stub?

Taxes, taxes, taxes!
Take home pay too low
who wants to know?

You want to see my papers?
My notebook? My poems
telling my story—

Papers with new laws
deny my existence
because some papers

don't tell it all
my dignity my pride is
not printed on *THOSE* papers

those papers will burn!
Why do you want to see my papers?

My Two Méxicos

There are two Méxicos I know,
the one where I grew up and learned many things,
about the north.

Where my parents were born
where I learned English as a boy,
where my umbilical cord is covered by that soil.

I learned to love what is mine
what mattered – and the culture
still in my blood.

The other México is the one I don't want to be part of—
poverty   corruption   class division
impunity   hunger   assassinations,

drug wars, marginalization. Where foreign capital dictates
what local politicians please to do,
and do it for money like whores.

Where the poor are dying, where the rich get fatter
where, wealthy foreigners
continue buying precious coastline.

México, pedophile and prostitution heaven
cheap vacation paradise.
"Mexicans are beautiful people"

as long as they don't cross the borderline.
Hypocrite politicians invent laws to keep them at bay
unwanted but essential. Lawmakers wish there were

an ocean from San Ysidro down to Corpus Christi.
Keep on wishing...
These are two countries

attached by a river linked like flesh and bone
like a young kid looking up to his big brother
wishing that some day He would become like Him.

Two Méxicos I know—
the one I love and remember,
and the one I don't   want   to   know.

c/s

Working the Fields

It is a dream—
I immerse myself in that dream which does not feel
like a dream, because I'm not dreaming,
I'm re-living what I heard before.

Back in the day, the migrant days a vanished past
but present at best when I smell the fertile soil,
aroma of the valley in the early morning.

The fragrance of the earth when rain vaporizes.
Swirls of hope from the hot ground up.
I breathe, breathe and breathe until my lungs can't hold such bliss

exhaling memories like rows of apple and orange trees.
Rows of plum trees, rows of lettuce fields, rows of strawberry fields.
Everything comes back, the sacks full, crates bursting with fruit.

Tomatoes, asparagus bundles, lettuce crates.
Migrant farmworkers filling cotton sacks heaping
breaking their backs from dawn to sundown.

Aching muscles, fragile, like dry sticks of fine crystal.
Dirty, thirsty, hungry men and women with soil on their hands.
A day's work for a day's pay with soil still in their fingernails dry.

Working the fields is the ultimate reverence man can pay to the land.
Retrieving the harvest.
Our land, their land, the land whose soil we walk.

Cuando no había fronteras / When There Were No Borders
From a conversation with the former US Poet Laureate Juan Felipe Herrera
Richard Hugo House, November 22, 2019

We talked about quelites, watercress and herbs
good for the body and mind and the memories
embedded in the fibers of acociles, esquites, elotes
and all that we left behind.

Not a coincidence but a cultural fact
when we learned that nuestros abuelos, padres,
tíos y primos crossed "la linea" to harvest the land
from the Yuma fields, Tulare's groves, Louisiana cotton

cattle and horses Colorado, Idaho, Nevada farms.
They worked the season and then went back
before snow and frost covered the ground.
Too cold en el Norte, heading South to sun-land

We agreed that en aquel entonces, back then
"Cuando no había fronteras", when there were no borders
they crossed, worked, and went back. That's it!
Back then "we were not shadows, now we walk through the shadows"

History has been forgotten. What was dignified then,
is now a criminal act, a death sentence equals the desire
to live, to be free, to be happy, to speak their mind.
We belong to this ancestral land.

Contract Number 127068

In 1944 the "War Manpower Commission" issued a proclamation to contract non-agricultural Mexican workers. My father and many men heeded the call, lured by the opportunity to work "del otro lado", on the other side of the border. He was single man who worked the silver mines in "Real del Monte" a silver town in the state of Hidalgo. I will never know his motivation to come to the United States. He passed away when I was twelve, but I can say; he saw the opportunity to earn and save his money to create a business upon his return. He signed the "Individual work agreement" in the city of Queretaro, Qro, Mexico the third day of July 1944, signed by G.A. Walls, contract agent which the contract refers to as the "Patron". The US Army enlisted every able young American man into the forces, leaving factories, businesses, manufacturing companies, infrastructure halted due to the lack of manpower. The war depleted factories from laborers and skilled workers to run the machines, thereby halting manufacturing of goods and services and the expansion of commerce routes. This War Manpower proclamation was seen as a way for Mexico to be involved in the Allied armed forces.

Even though the contract stipulates on Provision #16: "The Worker shall not be subject to discrimination in employment because of race, creed or nationality in accordance with the Executive Order N° 8802 of the President of the United States, dated June 25, 1941, they were subject to discrimination and mistreatment including lynching along the border. With much discrimination as was intended, the background checks took place. DDT was sprayed, an unstoppable *"sanitary measure"* the agents said. Treated and caged like animals, they surrendered to the "requirements" to work in the USA, among them: To be healthy and physically fit as stated in the certificate issued by the Mexican Health Department in accordance with the United States Public Health Service. If it was discovered that the worker was suffering from a heart, mental or venereal disease or had a chronic condition not contracted during or as a result of his employment in the United States, or if he has a contagious disease discovered while travelling from the point of origin to his destination in the USA, he was considered unfit. They were also required to live in the accommodations provided by the Patron. My father was one of those invisible men. I didn't have the knowledge as I do now about the abuse and mistreatment these men had to endure when they came to help out with the war efforts. World War II In so far, not a single radio station or digital media has mentioned anything about this fact of support by willing young Mexican Workers. Their pay was measly if you want to know, it was 0.30 cents per hour. I have one of his savings stubs from The Atchison, Topeka and Santa Fe Railway Company dated November 16th to November 30th, 1944 showing 10% savings out of that pay period. After his return, he never received those savings. I know my father worked with resolve to fulfill his life upon his return. I have a photo of my father with his buddies present as proof and Testimony of his contribution to the victory in World War II.

My father was a warrior too!

Migration is the story of my body.

-- *Victor Hernández Cruz, Poet*

Part II •• ome

Zatepan / Después / Later on

EL NORTE

Life / *Vida*

these days filled with lies	*mentiras,*
fear, intimidation smoke screens,	*humo*
nebulous particles we breath	*respiramos*
inhale deep, because we need	*aire*
air to live—	*vida*
the orange glow	*resplandor*
father sun, Tonatiuh	*sol*
remains in the center—	*el centro—*
while the planet floats	*flota*
we make the earth turn,	*vueltas*
the rhythm of our heartbeat	*latido*
our pulsing heart	*corazón*
the size of a postcard stamp	*estampilla*
stuck, on the map	*pegada*
of our existence	*existencia*
the cycle repeats itself	*se repite*
the cycle begins once more	*continua*
when night falls, we rest	*descansamos*
our soul,	*alma*
to see the light	*luz*
the new wind of change,	*viento nuevo*
the new day.	*el nuevo día*

It is Dangerous to Have Dark Skin

we "could be criminals"   when WE speak our mind
we "could be violent"   when WE protest police brutality
we "could be thieves"   when WE demand Justice!
we "could have a weapon" when WE like to live in peace
we "could be illegal"   when WE want to be free!

because—
we "look suspicious when we wear hoodies"

because
we "are up to no good"

because
we "wear strange clothes"

because
we "look dirty from working all day"

because
we "don't look like regular folk"

We are dangerous—
because; we look different.

Growing Up in America

Remember...

the classroom full of kids with different colored skins
learning the difference between a noun and a pronoun.
Remember how innocently everybody used to play—
together, in the schoolyard?

Remember—

how you shared your lunch and others shared theirs with you?
Different flavors, different tongues.
Now you are in high school — in a different classroom.
With different faces, same-colored skins.

Remember,

how it didn't matter where you came from?
the sound of your voice—
and your indigenous features were not a subject of repugnant
scrutiny and criticism?

Learning

from others the "differences" between races
why one ethnic group doesn't get along with others.
Notice that same color kids, hang together—
like worms in compost...

Now—

ostracized due to your skin color your name,
your features your other language.
How does that feel? You — get pushed—
to the end of the line your hair pulled by others.

They tell you:

"you are a *greaser* and a *wet back*, your dad washes dishes,
at a Mezkin restaurant
and your mother cleans toilets at juvie hall"
they mock you — playing your violin.

They tell you,

"go back! where you came from
don't speak your *"Espanish"* language
speak English!" There is no class
in the classroom.

Only

class divisions, ignorance, prejudice
based on racial differences.
Red man, Yellow man, Black, Brown, White ones too—
what happened to the innocence of the early years?

Everyone

learns the poisoned language of snakes.
They use nouns, pronouns and verbs to hurt others
with their serpent tongues bifurcated contaminated
diseased approach to the culture of hate.

Growing up in America

Nationalization

assimilation	feminization	constitution
concentration	masturbation	coalition
saturation	ejaculation	coalition
polarization	prostitution	evolution
gentrification	satisfaction	communication
population	connection	satiation
proliferation	reflection	modernization
discrimination	validation	simplification
repatriation	education	naturalization
repudiation	socialization	negation
immigration	indoctrination	vindication
consolidation	separation	retribution
deportation	manifestation	sedation
fascination	revolution	eradication
legalization	proclamation	irrigation
conciliation	emancipation	beautification
invasion	colonization	simulation
pollution	predomination	distribution
fumigation	evangelization	filtration
reflection	humanization	aggravation
confusion	contamination	in our nation

TO OWN A GUN DOES NOT GUARANTEE
P R O T E C T I O N
OH! BUT RELIGION
GIVES C R E D E N C E TO SUCH
I N D I G N A T I O N
BLESS THE B U L L E T, B L O W
THE S M O K E, SMITH & WESSON

american guns

scattered   bodies,   bullet   casings

people   running,

p   l   u   m   m   e   t   i   n   g

to   the   ground

uninterrupted   gun   blasts

agonizing   screams,

dark   blood   puddles

layers   of   skin   flown   by   the   wind

shadows,   broken   limbs

eyes   closed

Restful sleep   interrupted

radio   broadcasts

an   American   killing   Americans

on   his   own   ground

blood   blood   blood   more   blood

The   barrel   of   a   gun   holds

the   infinite   silence

of death

Wind

Invisible men
Stand outside
Home Depot
Only the wind
Knows
Their names

Sanctuary
For José Robles

His crime is—
his desire to live with dignity.
He is undocumented,
doesn't need a license to live,
is the anchor of his family.

A painter by trade, he wears an ankle monitor
sits on the concrete bench,
behind the iron gate
he doesn't want to be deported.
He smokes a cigarette.

Looks up to the sky seeking solace,
he watches the painters across 9th.
misses his family, his friends, watches TV,
he feels like a caged lion,
paces back and forth.

He stops—listens, to people talking out in the street,
lives off take-out,
he feels he is in purgatory.
He is in sanctuary, in the lilac basement,
sheltered in a sacred place a man lives

while he waits and waits.
Knows he cannot change his past,
he cannot defy ICE.
Doesn't want to risk his family,
gets horrible headaches.

Was assaulted, kicked in the head.
His body slammed on concrete,
lives in fear—
in fear for his daughters, alone with their mother.

The caged lion roars in silence.

He paces and paces and paces,
lives behind secure walls,
he feels like a prisoner,
whose only crime
is to be human.

September's Last Day

Church sanctuary,
stained glass and filtered light
children play violin, cello.
Century old songs with flair
striking every note on cue.

Fingers press strings
vibrato memorized process
contained in their young brains,
each artist bows
at the end of every song.

Meanwhile the homeless
file into the basement
as if entering purgatory
leaving behind dirty alleyways
full of filth.

No Psalms read at night
no Amen or Hallelujahs between the pews
only sleeping bags rolled out
to crash below the heavens
and the safety of the Holy Ghost.

Silent Silence
A poem for two voices

Silence	*quiet murmur*
Palpation	*silent heart*
Silent	*wind breeze*
Women	*walking*
Distant	*silence*
A thought	*evoked*
Silent wind	*quiet sails*
Silent shores	*silent waves*
Silent dawn	*silent warmth*
Silent trees	*wave*
Silent branches	*sway*
Silent birds	*glide*
Down, down	*in silence*
Silent hills	*silenced*
I close your	*silent eyes*
Your body	*silenced*
Lifeless	*silent*
Silenced	*sealed*
Silently	*I murmur*
A prayer	*of love*
In your right ear	*Silenced*

Corazón arraigado
For Magdalena Ruiz's kidney transplant fund raiser 3-24-2019
At the Hacienda San Pancho Gallery, San Francisco Nayarit, Mexico

Aquello que mantiene el flujo de la vida
líquido, coagulante.
Aquel líquido vibrante que lleva
la esencia del alma constante,
fuente de vida, semilla principal
de la raíz que palpita
ahora seca colgante mostrando a la luz
su áspera belleza triunfante.

Rooted Heart

That which sustains life's flow
coagulant, liquid.
Such vibrant liquid carries
the constant essence of the soul,
fountain of life, germinating seed
of the palpitating roots,
dried up, hanging, showing the light
of its triumphant rugged beauty.

Vines and Wind

Wet grass
wind, motors
children running.
I'm back
to the night my father
held my hand
across the park
where we sat.

That cement bench
still there.
Vines
draped over the line
my father's arm
draped over my back.

The wind
his soft voice
his words
distant chimes

"*I love you, your
noble heart*"

indelible
ripe as pears
his sweetness
waiting to
fall.

My father gone.
Late fall
I was twelve
too young
to learn what
he couldn't teach me,
to plant vines
to drape
like memories
like wind.

Mira!

Mira   mira   mira   mira   mira   mira   mira

    mira   mira   mira   mira   mira   mira

mira   mira   mira   mira   mira   mira   mira

    mira   mira   mira   mira   mira   mira

mira   mira   mira   mira   mira   mira   mira

    mira   mira   mira   mira   mira   mira

mira!

al cielo donde todo cambia
to the sky where everything changes

This Poem Doesn't Exist

Between the thin air and the clouds
only the sun is elemental.
Up here, there are no bones
or breathing lungs
no laments…
only silence.

At the edge of the universe
the twilight
without thorns or petals
takes shelter in the cloud's
shadow
oscillating its luminous veins

across the arterial plough
of its celibate
diaphanous inheritance
where it lays in the subtle
nakedness
of its own smoothness.

Such finesse pale and elusive
under the orphan veil
breaks the knot in an instant
at the sudden sound of the voice,
removing the veil
pouring its sweetness

in the abyss of the earth
at the moment in which
the transparent longitude
destroys the insomnia
crumbling down
when thunder screams.

Without a trace
the wounded clouds spew
their angry drops
on earth's soil nourishing
the flowers, the trees, the worms
and all living creatures.

Women Are

From Coatlicue to Sor Juana Inés
women from all ethnicities have walked
this earth with their tireless feet
giving birth, giving life.

Rigoberta Menchú Guatemala City,
La Soldadera, Las Adelitas guerrrilleras.
Frida Kahlo pintora, Cisneros escritora
Lila Downs cantora con su voz,

sings songs to all rich, poor, happy or not
desperate lament of love—
Pen in hand Castellanos writes poems,
black ink bleeding on paper white indelible as doves.

María Sabina mushroom priestess.
Women are sustainers, protectors peace makers
and warriors, beacons of humanity
Women are powerful!

Women have the wisdom of the creator they bear life.
Without women   men   cannot survive.
Women are the yin of life! Their nurturing and motherly love
make   men   out of children.

Women know what   we-men   don't.
Women have a golden aura, women shine.
Women have charming power, women change things.
Women give life!

Women give love.
Women are *curanderas*, healers
Women are shamans
Women can bring down the sun and the stars

if they want to—
Women are the beauty of the world.

The Shelter of Your Chest

Guard my backside from the thin knives
of their dreary eyes
guard me between azaleas and marigolds
guard me between wood and musk
in your misty meadow
guard me, between the roots of cedar and maple
in your snow-covered mountains
guard me burrowed in the wet sand
ocean waves brush
guard me between twilight and the early light
between mist and rain, thunder and storm
in the rainbow, guard me between azure and purple
guard me between the sheets of your bed
tucked in like balled socks
guard me from disdain
guard me—
guard me inside, outside,
over, under, beside your chest.

Let us guard each other from the fallible
keep the torchlight on, raise your red rose
I am your warrior.

Your Body

I want to surf your body
ride every curl, curve and crevice
I want to trace every tattoo
beginning with the rose's stem
on your ankle.

I want to entwine
the vine
running up
your thighs
with the tip of my tongue.

I want to lick the nectar
of your blossoming
love
one drop at a time
I will release the butterflies

in your womb.
I want to get lost in your hills
your valleys, your highways.
I need no compass
I will follow

the sparkle in your eyes
the stars in your hair
cascading down
your shoulders
your hips.

I'm seasoned wood

I want to burn
in your fire
of desire
let the blinding smoke

shroud our embrace.

Two Boats

if my lips were fire
I would consume you in less time
than the blazing fire would take
to devour the green logs of your youth

in silence   the male and   female cats
climb on our torsos
waiting for a nightly caress
while we sleep

you are on top of me like a cat
your hair silky as dawn
hot as the sunset
tempered as dusk

we move like two boats
anchored to the edge of pleasure
our lips rub with each grunt
and every kiss is, a heartbeat

Dos lanchas

si mis labios fuesen lumbre
yo te consumiría en menos
tiempo que la lumbre devoraría
los troncos verdes de tu juventud

en el silencio   el gato y   la gata
se montan encima de nuestros torsos
esperando una caricia nocturna
en nuestro remanso

tu estas encima de mi como una gata
tu cabello terso como la alborada
candente como el atardecer
templado como el anochecer

nuestros cuerpos se mueven como lanchas
ancladas a la orilla del placer
nuestros labios se rozan con cada
gemido, y   cada   beso es   un   latido

Three Words

Today was a storm-less day,
faint drizzle at best.
Tempered sunlight
front railing stained.

No UPS packages,
no bags left outside,
no messages on the phone,
no problems tonight.

Fresh veggies for supper
cooked down slow,
flavor of the land
and the hands that sowed the seed.

Those hands, tender hands
always give, even what they don't have.
Those soft hands belong,
to an angel in disguise

with golden hair and green eyes
to whom I say
every chance I get,
I love you—

all the time.

A man's reach should exceed his grasp, or what is heaven for?

-- *Robert Browning*

Part III ••• yeyi

Axcan / hoy / Today

AMPLITUDE

Poets' Temple

I would like to see a Temple for Poets
where every Sunday the sermon
begins with Walt Whitman's 'Leaves of Grass'
followed by Yeats 'A Dialogue of Self and Soul'
and William Blake's 'The Angel'

Ezra Pound will make the sharp distinction
between literary and esoteric traditions.
May Sarton will jump in to tell us how it is…

William Carlos Williams will debate her points.
Neruda will bring understanding
to the words we heard.
Meanwhile Federico García Lorca,
will stand in the pulpit, to tell us about 'La aurora.'

Cuando *"llega y nadie la recibe en su boca*
porque allí no hay mañana ni esperanza posible,
la luz es sepultada por cadenas y ruidos"

Solemn music invades the atrium
when the modern poets, the beats, walk in
like the Saints did at one time.
In the line we see—
Ginsberg, Kerouac, Marty Matz, Bukowski.

Books under their shoulders
ready to let the words   f l y   in the air,
the music in their voices filled the space

and all of us bowed down

to our muses floating in thin air
glorifying the words, sound,
metaphor and rhyme,
where poetry lives and shines!

Excuse Me Absent Poet but...

I wonder,
if you ever wrote anything
about the silhouette trees make
or the sounds unheard when instruments
are   played?   The   cries   of   hungry   people.
The snoring of alcoholics sleeping on doorways.
Torn knee ligaments, steam boiler ignitions.
Silent conversations in crowded malls.
Tapping shoes rhythmically
at the beat of jazz or blues.
Leaves on branches
High. Crows ear
s p l i t t i n g
h u bb u b.
C a t s
purring,
dogs
dreaming,
fish
breathing,
in the
water,
tanked,

silent.

Have you ever heard those sounds, dear absent poet?
I've heard them all
tonight.

Selecting a Reader

Cento poem composed with all the titles but 5 from Jim's New & Selected Poems
Carnegie-Mellon University Press 1978
(For James Bertolino on his birthday October 5th, 2019)

The Teacher selected the Snow Angel
Beyond the Storm As if Bound
In Liquid Moonlight.
The Night was Smooth but The Cold Room.
Day of Change when the Yellow Spring,
Spring Thaw: Fish, The Scavenge
Woke The Flower and the Barefoot Lover
The Landscape filled with Lizards and Gulls
Salmon Fishing, Boundary Bay,
That December Thirteen, Storms, Relentless
To The Hum, Seventeen Year Locust
created The Story of The Sacrifice Mom & Sally
made that day. Something Familiar, a Song for the Unborn
Extending Foreground The Marriage at Memorial Park at Sunrise.
The Veteran, The Baker were present
even the girl wearing The Red Dress
who said: I wish I Had a Packard, The Pleasure of The Italians.
After the Climb and Love's Body Consumed
Notes for an Elegy mentioned the Talisman
In the Portrait: My American Man all the Changes
expressed, The Blood Vision through the Blue Bottle.
Employed, I sold a Poem titled: The Pothole Sonnet
based On a Line by John Ashbery.

Twenty Cloves of Garlic at the Tree Top House
For Neil Chrisman on his birthday July 7th, 2020

Always expect the unexpected.

After a day of shimming,
       nailing, caulking things,
              the reward comes.

              An old friend, a good friend,
                  an exemplary man
                        celebrates his birthday today.

Family and friends gather six feet apart,
       walking on our own two feet
              to toast across the deck

              at the top of the tree house.
                  Despite the crisis, we sit here.
                      Obeying, complying, respecting

their being, their health,
       our desire to meet, mingle,
              and celebrate among friends

              whose friendship last for as long
                  as we can breathe.
                      Hopefully we may be able to give—

each other a tight hug,
       a very tight hug,
              an embrace that says:

              I love you man!
              I love you,
                  for being my friend.

White Feather

The spines of nopales are still embedded between my teeth.
I spat out the blood and vile stark memory of what was, unforeseen
future. The past that was, dwindling away smoldering candle flame
blown darkness prevailed and permeated the space. Lived, vacated,
abandoned quiet, silent, silence   sssh!,   sssh!,   sssh!—

Listen to their wings! flap flap, flap, flap the angels are here,
between you and me. I never believed 'Angels' could be real until
the day a white feather fell on that nightstand. Reminded   me,
the soul is weightless, while the body is heavy and the dreams are
heavier but tender in the dark. Sometimes they weep and scream
silent vision of a crying angel's face covered   under   the   gauze.

The secrets, the laments, the tears kept on caressing my face, while
I wept whispering their names, all the names of those who showed
me tenderness—

Your face, your voice, your disagreements across the table, devoid
of illumination. But who am I to judge you and them when   I   was
just a bystander in time—

Let the feathers fly, flutter until the morning dawn when you and I
and them will fly free, unbound, fluttering away like Monarch
butterflies.

Pirinola

En el huacal de la vida, nuestros sueños cuelgan
de un mecate como un tambache de ropa limpia
encima del burro de planchar, un montón
de tiliches y planes inconclusos. Aun así seguimos
caminando en nuestros huaraches
luciendo nuestros huipiles y guayaberas
con la cara al sol y con orgullo de ser
Mexicanos!

Siempre adelante evadiendo el chapopote
de la inmunda sociedad. Nuestros jacales y casas
rodeadas de nopaleras y huisaches
donde nuestras verdes milpas dan elotes,
chayotes, chiles y epazote, regalo de la tierra,
nuestras tierras. Listas para la pisca
bajo el ahuehuete del abuelo
disfrutaremos del aire limpio y puro.

Comeremos frijoles de la olla, pozole, chilaquiles,
tinga, nopalitos, mole, tortillas, tamales y
quesadillas de cuitlacoche mientras vemos
a nuestros chilpayates jugar a las escondidillas
echándose manchicuepas, comiendo paletas
volando papalotes, corriendo con rehiletes
jugando al trompo en el tambaleante
sube y baja de la vida.

La pirinola de la vida algún día...
se detendrá y dirá "Pierdes Todo"
y luego al petate.

Tapen mi cuerpo con mi mejor sarape
traigan a mi tumba cempazuchitl y pata de león.
Ése día el cenzontle y la chachalaca cantarán
canciones viejas parados en las ramas del pirul
más grande de mi tierra.

A New Star in the Darkened Sky
For my First son, Vaisnava Gosai Sánchez,
(June 11, 1984 – February 11, 2020)

We are a deck of cards someone else shuffled, we are thrown into the world, the
gamble of life.
We learn to walk, to live. Each step is a story and each story is a new star in the
heaven of our memory.
-Ruben Blades

I remember the day he was born
the years when the three of us
jumped and laughed at silly jokes,
the years when he would smell dandelions
because for a child everything is beautiful.

I remember, he loved to wear
my Mickey Mouse t-shirt.
Back in '88 he won the *"Cutest kid"* photo contest.

I remember—
He begot a daughter at 17
He tried to be a man on his own.
However the divorce separated us all.
He had a rough time in this world
he lost one of his younger brothers
Keshava Kumara under the Wyoming sun.

I remember—
the blown tire, tragic disaster
I remember :: I remember it all.
He was unharmed, but not his brother
now gone.

He was only eleven years young,
too young.

I remember—
the laughter, their made-up words
like "Sarkolaks" the ruler of the fable he wrote.
Horses, shields and swords
the aspiring king that wanted to save the world.

Death comes unannounced,
silently, in the light of day or in the darkest nights.

A child that never saw
the wonders of this world.
Now both join hands,
to once again, walk the thorny path.

Gosai's beautiful life didn't shine as I wish it had,
a victim of his own vice.
However, the void exists.

My wish is—
for his soul to cross with ease
guided by the light, energy and warmth,
of the candle lit
and his name uttered into the universe,
where the souls reside.
He needs all the light he can get,
to cross over to the other side.

The memories come back
like the sound of rumble strips
driving at night. Sometimes they sound
like living water dripping into the void
down the drain merging

into the whole and magnanimous
river of souls.

Where do they all go?

Rain drops drip and fall
wet grass, rocks, cement sidewalks.
Death is inevitable as it is, the end of life.
Everyone alive will testify
that it is not easy to live
the life we were dealt.

Not all of us were born under the same stars.
Some are brighter than others,
such mystery I can't define.

May his soul rest
I hope he will respond
when I call his name
Vaisnava Gosai Sánchez
Que Viva!

Quilted Memories

Tonight, I find myself sewing memories,
a blanket of discarded fabric—
thoughts, and worn-out feelings,
like old t-shirts sewn together
quilted.

Every night I throw that blanket,
over my decaying body.
Especially on the nights when my soul cries
and when the stars do not shine.
Oh!

Lamenting for the chasm I have created,
the unnecessary grief and sorrow
of those nights, more than one night
darkened feelings, repressed thoughts
a river of doubt.

I have skipped over deep puddles,
jumped across cold mountain streams,
to land on the green side
away from the nettles of my forgettable
past.

The future will always be there,
for those behind.
I cannot jump over the shallow
streams, of someone else's
life.

He gives me a hug. ▓▓▓▓▓▓▓▓▓. He likes me. ▓▓
▓▓▓▓▓▓▓▓ his girth makes him ▓▓▓▓▓▓▓▓▓
▓▓▓▓▓▓▓▓ endearing.

I sit on the deck ▓▓▓▓▓▓▓▓▓▓▓▓▓▓▓▓▓ The
water's brown. ▓▓▓▓▓▓▓▓▓▓▓▓▓▓▓▓▓▓▓▓
▓▓▓▓▓▓▓▓▓▓▓ RAW SEWAGE ▓▓▓▓▓▓▓▓▓▓
▓▓▓▓▓▓▓▓▓▓▓▓ Dusk comes, ▓▓▓▓▓
▓▓▓▓▓ over the swaying trees, ▓▓▓▓▓▓▓▓▓▓
▓▓▓▓▓ like a mild dog happy to be tied, ▓▓▓▓▓
▓▓▓▓▓▓▓▓▓▓▓▓▓▓

Noodles. Milk.

Freedom, I think: very nice.

▓▓▓▓▓▓▓▓▓▓▓ Buddy cooks eggs. They're good eggs.
▓▓▓▓▓▓▓▓▓▓▓▓▓▓▓▓▓▓▓▓▓▓▓▓▓▓▓▓
▓▓▓▓▓▓▓▓ Buddy and Mike fart with impunity, ▓▓
▓▓▓▓▓▓▓▓▓▓▓▓ lifting their butt cheeks. ▓▓▓▓
▓▓▓▓▓▓▓▓▓▓▓▓▓▓▓▓▓▓▓▓▓▓▓ Mike says
it's time to start pulling. ▓▓▓▓▓▓▓▓▓▓▓▓▓▓▓
▓▓▓▓ It's not easy ▓▓▓▓▓▓▓▓▓▓▓▓▓▓▓▓▓▓
▓▓ At nine we take a break ▓▓▓▓▓▓▓▓▓▓▓
▓▓▓ and have some bottled water. ▓▓▓▓▓▓▓▓▓ a
kingfisher pulls something out of the muck ▓▓▓▓▓
▓▓▓▓▓▓ and eats it ▓▓▓▓▓. Along the shore ▓▓ de-
caying ▓▓▓▓▓▓▓▓▓▓▓▓▓▓▓▓▓▓ bunkhouses ▓▓
▓▓▓▓▓▓▓. At noon we stop at one for lunch. ▓▓▓▓▓
▓ a filthy man digging up potatoes ▓▓▓▓▓▓▓▓▓▓

▓▓▓▓▓▓▓▓▓▓▓▓▓ says. "My wife's put out a heckuva
fine spread today. ▓▓▓▓▓▓▓▓▓▓▓▓▓▓ she does
great things with a spud. ▓▓▓▓▓▓▓▓▓▓▓▓ Go ▓▓
▓▓ see for yourself, by tasting some!"

From "CivilWarland in Bad Decline" by George Saunders 2016

Agringado

Alcahuetes fufurufos
chotean mis calcos
tacuches y mi ranfla.
Vengo de burque y hablo caló y qué!

Mi cantón se quedó en la capirucha
ahora lucho por la causa
chambeando lejos de los chirinoleros
filero en mano los chucos nos defendemos.

Cada quien su movida esé—
aguas con el zopilote
dale una sieta y una cervatana
pela chicharo y aguas con los mitoteros!

Solano Ruedas
c/s

Ya chales!

Tanto rollo con esa pinche plaga!
Todos prendidos y colgados, que gacho
The compas are not going to their jales
Sin varos no hay groceries ni tampoco Coronas
Modelos ni Tecates. Que onda carnal?
Esto esta de pelos hijo!
And then el sangrón
Anaranjado says: "don't worry, we got it"
Chales, 'che ruco mentiroso!
Nel hijo; that's not true
Ese fundillero y sus huele pedos
Can't stop it from coming.

Listen pendejo!

This mierda came from otro lugar
'che fulano fundillero y sus alachutes con marmajas
de lana payaseando picando placas ahí nomas
midiendo el aceite pelándo los dientes
ni calcos ni lisas tampoco esteisis.
Mejor descorchar el néctar de baco,
Hey Ese!   Chuco!
Destapa las Coronas carnal!
Préndele a doña diabla y chupale a las birongas.
Ya chitón! This will pass,   relax,   re-lax,   r e l a x,

r   e   l   a   x

r eeeee   llllll   aaa xxxx, m a n....

and watch me fly ese!

Quemando llanta

Órale vatos,
acá
on this side
of Aztlán
pónganse al alba
dejen de cabulear.

Chido tacuche,
buenos tubos en los calcos,
agarren su jaina ya!
Dejen de pestañear
pónganse chancla
el borlo va a empezar

rolas, birongas, refín
pisteando con Don Ramón
el ruco. La ranfla old Impala
quemando llanta
los locos tirando chancla
cumbia, simón, polkas de jalón.

Andrés pásame las tres,
quiero sentirme
aviadoooooor, Ese!
Tomorrow al jale
los varos hay que ganar
sin feria no baila el mono.

Dale gas Barrabas!
Échale vapor Nicanor
let's go cruise Whittier Boulevard.

Aguas con la chota
slow down man,
cool down in the hood.

East Los best
with the boys makin' noise, Esé!
Old school esteicis,
buttoned up lisa,
wango pants
next to the carruja
gold spoke wheels,
whitewall tires
pearl flake
and clear coat
air brushed—
Cuauhtémoc warrior.

Así mero, man!
Desde mi cantón,
Tlaltécatl les da bandera.
Hay nos vidrios
carnales y carnalas;
Wachenlé!

Reminiscing

Me and my Impala
cruising Hollywood,
tilting at Crenshaw
rear tail tilt at Western

left side up at Vine
past Cahuenga
all the way to Las Palmas
straight up at Highland

cops lurking for dragging
sparkling tail pipes
grinding,
bandanas hanging

Pendleton high button shirts
flowing.
Jose, Chuco, Rudy and me
riding *'ranflas'*

on lower than low
Hollywood streets.
We cruise the night
riding high in purple 1965

Chevy Impala
custom paint,
crushed velvet seats,
smooth ride—

the pride of the hood.

Tierra, El Chicano,
Third World music blasting
speakers loud

we scratch our way back
to Atlantic Boulevard
East Los *El Chante* homes!
Homies got to sleep too, *Ese!*
Hang over morning deal
menudo, pozole, birongas.
Tonight we cruise downtown
Main and Broadway our way

across the river.
Low riding, riding low
riding *'ranflas'*
on lower than low American streets.

Chevy Impala

Chicanos
Hitting the streets
Elevated shocks
Vintage cars
Yelling, órale vato!

Ideal custom cars
Mexican-Americans
Pump these up
Aztec motifs on the doors
Los Angeles. East Side
Aztlán!

Borinquen

Clave's rhythm takes me inward, in unison con *la sangre*, Taino blood.
I feel the hot sun kissing my skin, while Atlantic Ocean waves kiss, b*orinquen's* feet.
"La Isla del Encanto."

La Pachanga begins up on *Cañaboncito* Hills.
El ritmo de plena me sigue con Cuatro, Pandero y Güiro.
Pa' Ponce, Mayaguez, Bayamón y Caguas voy.
Vega Alta y Vega Baja también voy.

Palm trees sway with Salsa rhythm, Tito Puente's timbales beat,
echo from San Juan to *Nueva York*.
Tonight I'm gonna' play guaguanco y rumba like Ray Barretto,
'Mano Dura' did back in the hey-days of boogaloo con *Ritmo y Sabor!*

I will read Victor Hernández Cruz while sipping café *en pocillo*.
I walked Old San Juan's cobblestone streets to find *boricuas*
playing dominos. In my mind, I imagine Martín Espada *pregonando—*

en La Calle San Sebastián:
Alabanza! para ellos
Alabanza! para Puerto Rico
Alabanza! para Borinquen

A ritmo de Bomba me voy, pa' Carolina where Roberto Clemente was born.
Desde el Yunque mi Coquí canta happy midnight songs,
to serenade my tropical dreams.

Hector La Voe, *El Cantante de los Cantantes*; walked down
Calle Luna, Calle Sol. His distant voice, reverberates.
Look who's coming down Calle Cristo!
It is Willie Colón playing his trombone!

Mi china waits for me at the *Colmado con la fruta guindando*
near *Parada veintidós* where we had lunch *para dos.*
Asopao, tostones, pasteles y Mofongo de Concha con un palito de Ron!
Barrilito pol favol, Señol. Ay Bendito!

Up in El Morro's tallest tower my flag waves,
blessing *mi tierra santa, tierra pura*[1]
que con toda su hermosura
has given me infinite pleasure—

En Bellas Artes El Jíbaro Andrés Jiménez
cantando a Los Boricuas Ausentes:
"Viva mi Bandera, Viva mi Nación
Vivan los Boricuas que son Boricuas de Corazón."[2]

[1] *"tierra santa, tierra pura" is from Los Lobos song Maricela from Colossal Head 1996*
[2] *From: Andrés Jiménez "En Vivo, en Bellas Artes" Cuarto Menguante Records 2006*

Found Sonnets

Walking my dog one cold rainy night,
my two feet behind four paws ahead of mine,
we walked the parking lot without fright
or hesitation, knowing we were fine;

suddenly the dog stopped to find
muddied polyester fiber-filled headless
plush toys someone left behind:
dog, bear, rabbit, dolls abandoned, neat no less—

clothes strewn, toothbrush, hair brush all on the ground,
schoolbooks, notebooks, paperbacks' wet
discarded stories, fiction unfound.

I picked up a book, left others with much regret:
garbage to some, but *Shakespeare's Sonnets*?
Still dry for me to enjoy all the canzonets!

Dark Earth

Out of the dark and into the blue
Early light startles my sleepy mind,
Storms, earthquakes, toxic air, the sky no longer blue.

Sound of falling trees without a clue
Amazed and surprised to find,
Out of the dark and into the blue.

Mud slides, disaster, and death for more than a few.
God sent destruction to wipe out the humankind,
Storms, earthquakes, toxic air, the sky no longer blue.

Mother Earth surprised us, no one knew.
Soon will be our turn to find,
Out of the dark and into the blue.

Our lives darkened and no longer in the hue,
Slowly, the planet will come into a grind.
Storms, earthquakes, toxic air, the sky no longer blue.

Everything, every-thing all things will be askew,
A barren planet left behind,
Out of the dark and into the blue
Storms, earthquakes, toxic air, the sky no longer blue.

Hesperian Light
From the Moleskine notebook

Intrinsic silhouettes before my eyes
pine trees reaching to the powdered cloudless
blue sky to the west. Where I watch purple clouds
fighting the sun's last light burning through burnt orange
hues beyond the peaks Olympic peaks as the purple veils
fall   on the eyes of a dying man slowly   thinning slowly
shrinking slowly darkening until, until all the dark shadows
come out at the sound of the rhythmic chime playing song
of the late, late lazy summer wind to accompany the last light of day after His Majesty the sun
ran   off   beyond ocean lines, leaving   the   mountains
dark to witness the last glimmer hidden by the

m

o

o

n

l

i

g

h

t

Seattle Sky

L
a
c
k
l
u
s
t
e
r
sky
leaden
e a r l y
f l u o r e scence turbid
clouds hide diaphanous tinge blue
h u e o p a q u e s p l e n d o r
s m e a r e d   s p e c t r u m
misty veil draped across
the l a k e another
typical
S
E * E
A * A
T * T
T * T
L * L
E   D a y   E

Tahoma

I

North to south, east to west all roads lead to the mountain.
On sunny days the snow-covered peak is a glory
admired by tourists, the elderly and especially children.
Reached by many on expedition treks lead by horsemen;
magnificent creation enshrined by glimmering light,
at her feet; shrubs, plants small trees, tall pines in the forest.

II

On the good summer days we take trips to the forest
we stuff our backpacks with food, cameras, on our way to the mountain.
We drive above the clouds before we get to see the light once we reach Paradise!
By the spring meadows we breathe the air of glory.
We rely on the guidance and advice of the tempered horsemen who,
pay special attention to all, especially the children.

III

Our grandparents love to walk, but to run and play is only for the children.
There are natural waterfalls, cascades, and ponds in the forest.
We always obey the instructions of the horsemen,
because we do not want to get lost on the mountain.
We want to reach the top to witness the glory,
and proclaim we've seen the light.

IV

When dusk falls, we use lanterns, gas lamps, artificial light,
sitting by the fire we enjoy the warmth and joy of our children.
We tell family stories, adventures of fame and glory,
such are the pastimes of camping in the forest.
We take care of this natural beauty because we love this mountain,
as careful as we are, we still need the help of the horsemen.

V

They are tall, rugged, strong, good riders, they are the horsemen.
When they ride, they magically disappear into the light.
These men are the guardian spirits of the mountain,
they make sure humans like us behave respectfully, like children.
We appreciate and care for all the living beings in the forest,
preserving nature is man's glory.

VI

When I die, my body will be resting in the grave, but my soul will be in
full glory,
my good deeds will be honored by the horsemen,
guaranteeing that I will not end up in the black forest.
For my good karma and love of nature will keep me in the light.
I took care of my family, loved my wife, gave all my love to my children,
I lived in harmony and loved nature because - I have been to the mountain.

VII

In spirit I will always look up to the mountain to remind me of the glory
tender as children's smiles, stern as horsemen
gleaming in the sun light, illuminating the forest.

The earth is a living thing. Mountains speak, trees sing, lakes can think, pebbles have a soul, rocks have power.

— *Henry Crow Dog, American Indian Activist*

Part IV •••• Nahui

Xocotl Huetzi / cuando caen los frutos / When the fruit Ripens

THE PACIFIC NORTHWEST

My Experience at the Detention Center and Why
I Became Interested in Mentoring the Youth in Detention

There are seeds that are blown by the wind.
There are seeds that are planted by human beings.
Those seeds will grow into beautiful flowers and trees.
Those are the powerful seeds of knowledge mankind needs.

The seeds will germinate, throwing
roots expanded like fingers, grabbing hold of the earth.
The roots contain wellbeing, grandiosity,
wisdom, virtue, truth, pride, glory,

faith, harmony, agreement, disagreement
tranquility, ancestry, principle.
The roots will give way to the branches,
providing leaves, foliage, and fruit.

Reason, must be at the base of all that flourishes.
Think of the Dervishes' dance,
who whirl and whirl away.
There is a cosmic dance throughout the human forest,

where we encounter people from different places
and different faces.
I am one of those trees. I unraveled my branches—
to provide fruit and shelter to the seeds I planted.

These days I share fruit and shelter with the
youth in perilous situations. Compassion
and an open heart are the tools I use to help them
free themselves from the trauma and pain in their heart.

Poetry is the carving tool I use to remove,
the stumps that hold them down.
The words come out of their hearts like seeds,
germinating to create their own poems, poetry,

they didn't realize they already had.
When the young are praised,
their faces gleam like the sunshine in the early spring
Their poems are gems, strung together like diamonds,
after the rain.

Slam

The air behind these walls is heavy—
Here the minds mature faster,
young men and ladies separated,
without pride or prejudice.
Their scared skins, punctured flesh healed.
Black, red, yellow, brown, and white skins shot at,
punched, kicked. Their broken bones and spirits,
sheltered, confined.

A cement slab, two blankets and a pillow.
Cold cinder block walls frame the steel doors.
Some have inscribed their names, symbols,
numbers, secrets on those walls.
Everyone has a story to tell…
Encaged, separated, rejected from society,
everyone wonders how long their sentence will be.
The number on their wristband tells their story.

There are no restful weekends here, no birthday parties
or fun Friday nights. In detention, the days are l o o o o n g e r.
Only their minds can escape the monotony by reading,
writing, fantasizing, healing their mistakes.
Too young to hold a gun, old enough to die.
Patiently, time will pass while they persevere,
building the promise to themselves: "to be righteous"
to overcome their sadness and suffocation.

To show the world they don't deserve this isolation.
They examine their flaws while they sleep,
to restore their broken souls.

To wake up with the sound of the chirping birds
perched up on the highest bows.
To breathe the air of freedom, to step away from the threshold,
and hear the heavy door   **SLAM!**
For the last time.

National Poem in Your Pocket Day
April 30th 2020

We are the human forest
where all the trees
are different.
Yet we all share
the same sun
the same air
the same rain
the same soil
where all
our roots connect with each other
We are the human forest.

Kubota Garden, Seattle

There is a conversation in the silent garden.

Laceleaf Japanese maple whispers stories

in summer moonlight to the azaleas and rhododendrons.

Camellia blossoms by the stone vase glow, dazzle waves of pale green and red.

Burning bush leaves remind us winter is coming.

Two stone bridges united across the pond

resemble unity—over their reflection,

like humans crossing bridges walk the hidden paths,

sending forget-me-nots to their familial pink fallen petals.

In the garden, the sun yearns to cross the moon bridge,

and merge with the heart bridge, covered in snow.

Here all the flowers speak a different language.

Each petal, a different story.

Yet, all share the same soil, same sun, same air.

Plants and trees living in harmony, like humans should be.

across the path, guarded by twisted trunks and the necklace of ponds.

The beauty of the garden reflects the beauty of all living things.

Kumbh Mela for the Crows

(At the Meadowbrook Pond, North Seattle)

Sunday morning bathing gath
Kumbh Mela for the crows
away from daily detritus,
prosody when they call.

Ritual caw-caw cawing
again and again in response
raucous chorus
chasing ducks

across the pond
noisy spectacle, unique—
to black corvidae.
They dip their heads

in the water,
standing at the shore
like pilgrims by the Ganges
offering Ganga to Surya.

Crows don't know anything,
spiritual beyond their black
feathers, blacker than
the pupils of their eyes.

Orca Whales, Jewels of the Salish Sea
Inspired by Alfredo Arreguin's Twilight painting

I
Abundant salmon for the Orca whales, porpoises, sea lions, otters.
He sang of the restless seas where the great whales
Live, play, feed, reproduce in the inland waters of the Salish Sea.
Eagles watch them swim entangled in polluted waters.
Quileute and Makah hunters know *"Schelangen,"* they respect their obligation.
Undeniably, they are starving. Oil companies drilling, overfished salmon.
A long time has passed, 34 years to be exact, but the
Humans love to watch them.

II
Swooshing and crashing showing their dorsal fin.
Lummi nation has a sacred obligation to the Orca whales
feeding them, keeping them from starvation, emaciation and death.
swooshing and crashing showing their dorsal fin.
Alfredo watches the whales travel the Salish Sea
their playground and feeding grounds
swooshing and crashing, showing their dorsal fin.
from the Twilight above the water to the blue darkness beneath
the sea, the horizon stirs somber clouds across the muted sky,
swooshing and crashing.

III
Our desire to eat their food, and the dams holding the salmon back,
not enough food for the orca to survive.
Swooshing and crashing showing their dorsal fin.
Salmon dwindled due to climate change, pollution, container ships,
yachts and illegal fishing. Distant swoosh and a faint splash

reflect their majesty on the rippled water, trying to survive. Orca whales are the jewel of the Salish Sea.

Tieton's Bounty

There is a hidden place atop the yellow hills,
where poems and apples grow
orchards as far as the eye can see.

Black-billed magpie wings flapping
dogs running, chipmunks jumping,
raccoons eating fallen apples and the casual skunk,

may be a distraction, but certainly not for the poets.
They sit cross-legged under the trees.
Poets writing on spiral notebooks,

sweet poems amidst the pink ladies,
red delicious, sweet like limericks and sonnets.
Up there lies the hidden place,

where poems and apples grow
honed down, shaped under the sun.
Fluttering leaves fall like words,

onto their notebooks, poetic words grown.
Poems infused with apple fragrance,
crisp clean air, gentle as the wind,

born under the sun,
and the urgent river
below.

Bountiful Burien
City of Burien Poet in Residence program 2018-2019

Wholesome winds blow across the Salish Sea,
the city stands unsullied, while anxious waves
crash against the rocks untamed shore
as seen from Poet's Nest.

The Lushootseed people knew their natural treasures,
revered and protected the old-growth forest,
and their hunting grounds. Along the Duwamish, tended
cranberry bogs in the riparian waters.

Nestled in briny air, old trails and winding roads
spread this city from the magnificent valley
Michael Kelly viewed,
Sunnydale still its name.

Jacob Ambaum hacked the early roads in 1909,
now First Avenue cuts through the city
north to south, like an arrow in flight.
West of the Boulevard, there is a glacial spring

that feeds Burien Lake, pristine—
beyond the shadow of the Needle, glass towers,
loading cranes and jungle to the north
where ferries cruise from Vashon to the mainland.

Olde Burien shows vestiges of the early days
made old by time, we still adore that rusty,
rusty old sign for Tin Shop plumbing supplies
and Hayes Feed Country Store still open

for urban shoppers who still farm. Ambaum Boulevard,
a testament between modest and affluent homesteads.
Winding roads lead to the shore where luxury homes
watch the sun set across Puget Sound.

In Burien, people speak the language of food
Vietnam Pho, Thai curry, Oaxacan mole,
Italian meatballs, Tortas Locas, Australian meat pies,
Greek lamb, and Nepalese Thukpa soup.

Go ahead; I will see you at Smarty Pants,
for coffee. And later at 909 for a glass of wine!
From Three Tree Point to Manhattan
across Five Corners up to Boulevard Park

we revel in Duane's Garden patch to watch
the colors bloom beneath the Flight Path.
From all points, Shorewood, then south to Seahurst Park.
Burien; this land of dreams, watches the world fly in and out.

Just west of ninety-nine, Burien's indelible history shines
like sunlight through the center of Helios Pavilion,
it's green spears point to Tahoma and The Mother of Waters
waits, while the clouds evaporate.

Seola beach gushes with light, and Seahurst Park
a destination at the very end of Shorewood Drive.
Burien is a place of destiny—
awaiting all with open arms.

Embracing Redmond

From East to West the splendor of Redmond grows.
Their mission developed by its people's civic pride.
Here, professionals grow, beginners succeed.
Technology is a wealthy benefactor. The world gathers here,
a tiny dot on Washington state's upper corner.

West of Redmond across the Evergreen Point Floating Bridge,
the automated jungle rises far away from Bear Creek,
or Salmonberg as it was known in yesteryears.
The land of fishermen and loggers where Luke Mc Redmond lived.
Vestiges of the old Eastern Railway remain,

now signals park in the center of town.
Redmond celebrates its people and nature,
where the Sammamish River becomes a lake.
In Redmond, culture, art, languages and all the flavors
come to our table, along with music and dance.

Bharatanatyam, Bhangra, Kabuki, Jinta Mai,
Jarocho, Ranchero, Cumbia, Mambo, and Bomba too.
We dance, dream and remember, the roots left behind.
From the micro-soft to the mighty strong, like a Genie,
lifting all through technology, sculptures, poetry, and popular art.

We honor the Lushootseed people, guardians of this land.
Along the Sammamish river following the bike trail,
in spring and summertime. June to September
when the weather is dry, have a picnic, with the Poets in the park,
enjoy the art at So Bazaar.

While November is wet,
December is full of lights.
A flake or two of snow can add charm
to the lighted trees in the parks.
Redmond is the soulful place to be, all year round.

The Redmond Way

The air we breathe sustains us.
We need clean air to live,
to create, to love, to be.
None of us choose to be exposed.

However—
people are dying from breathing.
Unknown germs, silent, invisible
intangible, undetected.

World war without bullets
bombs, gases, but plain air.
Only we can save ourselves,
from ourselves.

All of us miss touching, hugging,
socializing. We will live to do that again.
The message is clear: wear a mask,
protect yourself and let others live.

The relentless virus disturbed our lives.
However we heed the message to survive.
Redmond citizens band together,
we will conquer, we will survive.

Life Precious Life!

In remembrance of the tragic event in Lake City 3-27-2019
"In the End We Are All Light" Liz Rosenberg American Poet

Ordinary Wednesday afternoon
quiet routine disturbed.
Cars, buses humming along
Sand Point Way over from Lake City
coming and going, shopping,
perhaps out for a game of pinochle.
Quiet routine disturbed, obliterated
by a drunken rampage
a day we don't want to remember.
A day that will remain embedded
in the fibers of our memory—
Sliced by helicopter blades, in the air.
Sirens cried and people screamed
woken up from the afternoon routine
by the gun blasts around the bend.
Powder smell, windows shattering
scattered glass, tires screech
a sound never heard so close.
Shocking, un-nerving — a warning.
Life's fragility, unexpectedly ending, disturbed.
Moments that live in the flesh of the survivors.
Deborah Judd, teacher, Eric Stark, bus driver
who like a wounded angel
drove the bus away from danger.
Their bodies still harbor the now cold lead.
We revere the memory of those who perished
Richard T. Lee—
Robert Hassan's ashes at the root of the oak tree.

Innocent citizens, neighbors, friends and passers-by.
Why?! We ask ourselves why…
Fragile as china, strong as steel
we remain friendly, watchful
active neighbors looking out for each other
this is the Lake City Way, the only way.
Life precious life! In Cedar Park, everyone
shares the same air, the same sun, the same rain,
living in harmony on the same earth.

The following five poems are part of a Public Art Project
by the City of Shoreline, WA

Vertebrae

"We don't see thing as they are, we see them as we are"
–Anais Nin

There is a place in the Northwest
where you will find a bridge, an overpass

resembling the spinal column of an ancient giant whale.
Enter the empty space devoid of marrow, sinew,

blubber and flesh. Devoid of muscles and nerves.
Only large bones around you, above you, beside you.

North to South to East to West
the wind carries the rumbling noise

raised from trucks and cars the ground below.
Bent metal pipes and chain link mesh

form the canopy to keep suicidal jumpers and
rock throwers safe on the path across I-5.

The days before the pandemic, traffic abound,
milk and fuel tankers, more trucks and motor bikes,

jam-packed, today traffic is less but the noise prevails.
I look up to the blue sky across the protective mesh

resembling fish nets, stockings worn by vedettes.
This overpass resembles the innards of a prehistoric

giant whale where walkers and bikers cross over
inside a whale's millennial vertebrae.

Vértebras

"No vemos las cosas como son, las vemos como somos"
–Anais Nin

Hay un lugar en el noroeste
donde se encuentra un puente, un paso elevado

que asemeja la columna vertebral de una antigua ballena gigante.
Entré al espacio vacío desprovisto de médula, tendón

grasa y carne. Desprovisto de músculos y nervios
sólo huesos grandes a mi alrededor, por encima y a los lados.

De norte a sur a este y oeste
el viento lleva el ruido retumbante

que se levanta de los carros y camiones.
Tubos de metal doblados y mallas de eslabones de cadena

forman el dosel para prevenir que los suicidas brinquen y
los maldosos tiren piedras sobre el puente que cruza la I-5

El tráfico abundaba antes que llegara la pandemia,
transportadores de leche y combustible, más camiones y motocicletas,

atascado, hoy en día el tráfico es menor, pero el ruido prevalece.
Miro hacia el cielo azul a través de la malla protectora

que asemeja a las mallas usadas por las vedettes.
Este paso elevado asemeja las entrañas de una prehistórica

ballena donde ciclistas y caminantes cruzan el viaducto
dentro de las vértebras milenarias de una ballena gigante.

Playball! (COVID-19)

Today I saw a lonely ball behind the cedar tree
at Hamlin Park while walking my dog.
I picked the ball up and stood on top
of the pitcher's mound while I looked around,

the empty field, the empty bleachers and
the lonely ball on my hand. I thought:
Today is a great day for a ballgame
Two rivals will compete for a spot.

Playoffs ahead, mid-summer fest
All Star Game, Home Run Derby
'Take me out to the ball game'
Sings the crowd, 7th inning stretch.

And what a stretch for the Dodgers
Vince Scully said, Chavez Ravine
6 - 4 - 3 Double play!
8 - nothing Dodgers on top.

However team COVID has 19 players on the field.
"We will win" Vince screamed!
A sea of Blue blood cheers
for the day we will play baseball again!

Today, the diamond is empty.
Only the crows came out,
while the red stitched ball waits and waits
under the sun above the fine combed dirt.

Pitcher's mound, bleachers,

bases empty. No one in sight
The ball waiting for someone's hands
to throw it up and yell:

"Play ball!"
But not right now.
Wear your MASK, wash your paws,
don't spit sunflower shells around.

Be safe, I'll see you at the
BALLPARK!

¡Pleibol! (COVID-19)

El béisbol es un ballet sin música. Drama sin palabras –Ernie Harwell-
Para Patrick R. Duff Su vida continúa en nuestras historias 2010

Nadie vino a oler el pasto recién cortado en los jardines
brillando con la lluvia temprana y la luz del alborada.
Tiza fresca por todas partes, solo silencio en las gradas.
Montículo de lanzadores, arcilla roja embalada, tope trasero listo,
el día de apertura ya pasó, pasmados por el COVID-19.

No hubo práctica de T-ball, no hubo pequeños héroes corriendo las bases
¡Pleibol! Grito detrás del home plate, el árbitro contando
Bolas buenas, bolas malas, bolas de foul y bolas perdidas
toques rodando con agonía lenta justamente fuera de la tiza.
Abalorios de rocío, bolas de colores objetos redondos que nos recuerdan

de aquellos juegos, cuando *Bob y Lucille Lee* aplaudieron a sus hijos
después de anotar un jonrón en el parque, mientras que *Lucas Shiner*
mantenía la puntuación en la tarjeta de juego.
El Rey de los deportes se juega con estilo, velocidad y un buen ojo.
Recuerden que *Dean Griffith* dijo: *"mantén tu ojo en la pelota"*

de lo contrario la pelota mantendrá tu ojo, "mira pa' riba!"
Deja que el cuero atrape las bolas, que atrape la pelota
navegando a través del cielo entre los cedros, los pinos,
arce y abetos, cornejo y aliso. Un jonrón distante que
encontrará refugio en los bosques y arbustos de Hamlin Park.

Smothered by Nature

Reverence for nature is compatible with willingness to accept
responsibility for a creative stewardship of the earth.
–Rene Dubos

Along the path flanked by logs
ferns, shrubs, greens, twigs, and fallen trees
aging forest brings peace, a respite
within the raucous sounds of city streets

Maple leaves intrinsic shadows cast their story
upon the undergrowth and the shallow stream.
Long ago man tried to plow the tree
abandoned the machine next to the young trunk

Along the way where metal succumbed,
where nature prevailed constricting metal,
rims, axles, transmission rods,
crows echoing the silent sound of time

Devouring the object, tractor at the roots,
twisted rusted metal immobile
rusted hoe, conquered by the years
of prolific natural growth

Mystery and beauty in both, tree and machinery
telling the story above the ground exposed.
Nature's resilience an open heart showing
its strong roots and might to survive.

Sofocado por la naturaleza

La reverencia por la naturaleza es compatible con la voluntad de aceptar
la responsabilidad del cuidado creativo de la tierra.
—Rene Dubos

A lo largo del camino flanqueado por troncos
helechos, arbustos verdes, ramas y árboles caídos
el bosque ancestral trae paz y alivio
dentro de los sonidos estridentes de las calles de la ciudad.

Las hojas del arce proyectan sombras intrínsecas
de su historia sobre la maleza y el riachuelo.
Hace mucho tiempo el hombre trató de cortar el árbol,
abandonó la máquina al lado del joven tronco.

En el camino donde el metal sucumbió,
donde la naturaleza prevaleció apretando el metal,
llantas, ejes, barras de transmisión,
los cuervos le hacen eco al sonido silencioso del tiempo.

Devorando el objeto, tractor en las raíces,
metal oxidado, retorcido inmóvil
azada oxidada, conquistada por los años
del prolífico crecimiento natural.

Misterio y belleza tanto en el árbol como en la maquinaria
contando la historia por encima del suelo expuesto.
La resiliencia de la naturaleza, un corazón abierto que muestra
sus raíces fuertes, y poder para sobrevivir.

Ode to an Oak Tree

"When the oak is felled the whole forest echoes with its fall, but a hundred acorns are sown in silence by an unnoticed breeze"
—Thomas Carlyle

Acres of aging grand trees on the lower ground
boughs bending, rising and falling with the wind,
randomly sinking and fainting responsive bird songs
dry ground covered with heart-shaped leaves and twigs.

At night, the trees on the higher ground cast
their shadow under the clear moonlight.
Your branches blown by the east-west wind,
secrets told when the birds can't sleep.

Full moon filled with countenance, dense,
murky clouds, wreaths of fragrant pines.
Oak and Cedar limbs swish with the wind brushed,
your very old mystical greatness stands.

Looking at the stars and the gorgeous clouds
in summertime your sun-drenched splendor.
Shelters birds hanging on your moist branches,
crows, blue jays, chickadees and eagle nests.

Nakedly standing in spring your dormant roots
thaw below the frozen ground.
Do not say that the roots are weak,
These roots are strong, the very roots of being.

Oda a un roble viejo

"Cuando el roble es talado todo el bosque le hace eco a su caída, pero cien bellotas son sembradas en silencio por una brisa inadvertida"
—Thomas Carlyle

El valle está lleno de acres de grandiosos árboles ancestrales
el viento sacude las ramas, arriba y abajo casi doblándose.
Las aves responden con canciones al azar que se hunden y desmayan
en tierra seca cubierta de ramas y hojas en forma de corazón.

De noche, los árboles en cerro proyectan
su sombra bajo la clara luz de la luna.
Tus ramas agitadas por el viento de este a oeste,
secretos que se cuentan cuando los pájaros no pueden dormir.

Luna llena con rostro de tristeza, densas
nubes turbias, fragrantes guirnaldas de pino.
Las ramas del roble y cedro crujen con el viento
cepillando tu infalible antigua grandeza mística.

Mirando las estrellas y las hermosas nubes,
en verano, tu esplendor empapado por el sol
da refugio a las aves que cuelgan en tus ramas húmedas,
cuervos, carboneros, arrendajos azules y nidos de águila.

En la primavera tus raíces latentes desnudamente
se deshielan, por debajo del suelo congelado.
No digan que las raíces son débiles,
estas raíces son fuertes, las mismas raíces del ser.

Greensward

Treat the earth well. It was not given to you by your parents... it is loaned to you by your children, Kenyan Proverb

Where the pavement meets the gravel road,
      leaves of grass and dandelion moons grow.

The open meadow opens to Western Hemlock,
      Pacific Madrone,

Black Cottonwood trees release translucent fuzzes
      twirling, falling down on nursing log sustaining life.

New saplings grow within the wounded tree,
      trunk leaning toward the sound

of the shallow stream where blackberry bushes,
      ivy, tall grass live.

Up above the canopy Spotted Towhee sings
      while crows and swallows fly from branch to branch

a symphony gleaming lulled by the breeze weaving,
      soft emotion warmth of the early spring.

And the birds sing, melodious noise along
      the luminous path across the open meadow.

Slow walk around the edge, step by step
      meditating on the tinkling dewy grass,

the glowing verdant leaves, a green oasis
      away from the rumbling sound of city streets.

Césped

Trata bien la tierra. Tus padres no te la dieron... tus hijos te la prestaron,
Kenyan Proverb

Donde el pavimento se encuentra con la grava
el césped y las lunas de diente de león crecen.

El prado abierto le da paso al Cicuta Occidental,
y también al árbol Madrone del Pacífico.

Los árboles de algodón negro liberan su pelusa translúcida
girando, cayendo sobre el tronco decadente que mantiene la vida.

Nuevos árboles crecen dentro del árbol herido,
tronco inclinado en dirección hacia el murmullo

del riachuelo donde los arbustos de moras,
hiedra, y yerbas altas crecen.

Por encima del dosel el Towhee manchado canta,
mientras que los cuervos y las golondrinas vuelan de rama en rama.

Una brillante sinfonía adormecida por la brisa tejiendo,
tiernamente la emoción de la temprana primavera.

Y los pájaros cantan, ruido melodioso a lo largo
del camino luminoso que atraviesa el campo verde.

Caminando lentamente a lo largo del borde, paso a paso
meditando en el rocío de la hierba tintineante,

las brillantes hojas verdes semejan un oasis verdoso
lejos del ruido estruendoso de las calles de la ciudad.

Sargent Sunny, My Homeless Friend

Every now and then when I walk my dog
Ranger at night, it could be autumn,
or the long dark rainy winter nights.

May 29th, is a far cry for sun to be had.
Sunny Sgt. told me tonight that he's been sleeping
outside, inside the Honey Bucket!

Out by the open yard where one night
a M*^#@!* F%*$#@! kicked-in the door cuz'
he wanted to pee!

Sunny said:
(remembering his Viet-Nam days)
I'ma kill you M*^#@!* F%*$#@!

you ain't gonn'a piss on me tonight
you F%*#@r!
He looked at me,

sunglasses below his nose and said pointing
his finger at me: you only got 90 seconds
to redeem yourself and bow down

to Jesus Christ!
I asked why? Not me I replied,
I know Jesus, he's my friend.

He continued ranting
about the way he got kicked out,
from the shelter he was in and the girl

he knew there,
who might the mom—
of his new child.

Sunny Sgt.! rest assured,
that as-long-as I know you are here,
you will always be the light,

shining in my mind.

before I'm gone

before I'm gone I want to visit
all the places that hold
memories of my youth

before I'm gone
I want to hug my friends
and squeeze their hands

before I'm gone
I want to see my sons
and my daughter once more

before I'm gone
I want to hear my poet friends
read their best work

before I'm gone
I want to touch the temple stones
aztec   mayan   olmec

before I'm gone
I want to visit my father
and my mother's grave

before I'm gone
I want to write
one last poem

before I'm gone
I want to have the last dance
with my loving wife

before I'm gone

ENDNOTES

Renato Leduc 1897 - 1986

Leduc, son of a French father and a Mexican mother, served as a signalist in Francisco Villa's *División del Norte*. Studied law at the Universidad Nacional de México. He wrote poetry, stories and chronicles. He traveled to Paris where he met several surrealistic writers. Leduc was a good friend of Elena Poniatowska, Federico Cantú, Luis Cardoza y Aragon, Octavio Paz and Agustín Lara, as well as of María Félix, to whom he was probably married.

AUTHOR'S NOTE

After my first book was published, I was surprised, elated by how many people were waiting to read what they've heard from me over the years on the open mic sessions all across town, up and down on the I-5 corridor as well as on the other side of the cascades in eastern Washington. I can safely say that I was the only "Latino" bilingual immigrant poet reading around town.

Well, it's been eight full years since my first book and I'm delighted to share with you my newest work.

My objective is to embrace my roots, my culture, my family and my purpose. Which is teaching, mentoring, sharing with youth what I've learned about poetry over the years. We need what the living planet is giving us, therefore it needs to be protected and revered. The inclusion of the Nahuatl language is to honor the history behind me. The language of my ancestors, the language I inherited and the language I speak where I live.

The poems in this book move from south to north recounting the experiences and visions of the time as seen on TV. Included are the stories from my uncles and some cousins who were migrant workers in their youth. Such is my experience and the reason why I migrated to the USA. "El Norte" where everything is prosperous, happy and magnificent.

Blame it on the TV Shows of the time (1960's), starting when I was five and through the influence of rock music and the cultural changes all over the world at the time. 1968 defined my outlook on life. Joan Baez, Victor Jara, Violeta Parra, Jose de Molina, Mercedes Sosa and Daniel Viglietti inspired me to write my first poem in 1972.

Renato Leduc was the first poet I ever heard. He was one of the celebrities that used to frequent my father's Restaurant "El Califa" a block away from Plaza Mexico, the biggest bull fighting ring in the world.

I feel this collection is part memoir, accomplishments, frustrations and overall joy for living and loving the people with whom I've crossed paths. I hope you enjoy reading part of my story.

Poetry sustains my soul. Family and friends are my lifeline. Inspiration is a gift and sharing with others is the biggest honor I could have ever imagined.

ABOUT THE AUTHOR

Raúl Sánchez is a Seattle-based author and mentor of bilingual poetry. His previous book "All Our Brown-Skinned Angels" published by MoonPath Press, launched his name into the roster of published poets. His cultural background allows him to use passages from his early life in México City and apply the lessons learned in his work. Since retirement, he has volunteered at the King County Juvenile Detention Center mentoring incarcerated youth through the PONGO method. His mentoring in the schools (WITS and Jack Straw Cultural Center), has been essential to his poetic growth because as he put it "The youth see the world differently than him," therefore he learns from their outlook. Raúl is an avid spiral thinker, driving in a straight line then suddenly turning left or right, but never loosing the reader in the detour. Raúl is a self-taught poet who keeps on writing, teaching, helping the youth, and reading in public, allowing his voice to carry the words like dandelion fuzzies into the ears of those who listen. For more information please visit www.rsancheztlaltecatl.com and www.picturesofpoets.com.

ABOUT THE ARTIST'S COVER ART

Fulgencio Lazo, painter and printmaker, works predominantly with acrylics on canvas at his studios in Seattle and in his hometown of Oaxaca, Mexico. He has had more than 50 solo shows throughout the United States, Mexico, and Japan, and has numerous pieces in public collections. He has worked for nearly three decades to promote and grow the Latino artistic and cultural scene in Seattle, most recently co-founding Studio Lazo, a cultural hub for Latino art, music and poetry.

http://fulgenciolazoart.com

ABOUT THE GRAPHIC ARTIST

René Julio, a Seattle based artist born in Mexico City, graduated from Universidad Nacional Autonoma de México in Visual Arts. His work has been presented in several exhibits in México City and throughout the country. Approximately twenty years ago, he migrated to the USA. His work has been included in several group and solo exhibits across the US and Mexico. He volunteered at "Casa de Artes" and "Taller Mexicano para La Cultura y Las Artes". He was part of the "Day of the Dead" celebrations at the Seattle Center House and has painted over twenty murals in the Seattle Area including two at Washington Middle School.

FB: @renejulioart